# CHANGING
# SCARBOROUGH

## PAUL CHRYSTAL

FONTHILL

Fonthill Media Limited
www.fonthillmedia.com
office@fonthillmedia.com

First published in the United Kingdom 2014

British Library Cataloguing in Publication Data:
A catalogue record for this book is available from the British Library

ISBN 978-1-78155-254-4

Typeset in 9.5pt on 12pt Mrs Eaves Serif Narrow.
Typesetting by Fonthill Media. Printed in the UK.

# INTRODUCTION

Scarborough was, and is, Britain's first seaside resort, and one if its most celebrated and finest. A reflection of its heritage, popularity and photogenic quality is seen in the number of books published on the town, many of which repeat similar, by now very familiar, views, old and new. *Changing Scarborough* takes and fresh and original approach, tracing the development of the town from Roman signal station, Viking conquest, medieval fortress and fashionable spa, through two destructive world wars, its role as a shipbuilding and fishing port to the renaissance resort it is today with its garish, thrilling sea-front entertainments, its prestigious Spa Centre, and Alan Ayckbourn's world famous Stephen Joseph Theatre.

Along the way, 200 images old and new—many of which have rarely been seen—depict a town constantly in transition—fisherwomen and fishermen, press-gangs and smuggling, the famous castle, pierrots and Punch, lighthouse and lifeboat, bombardment and blitz, fun fairs and fun palaces, stunning hotels, and rare sight of a vision of the future for Scarborough derailed by the Second World War. We get first-hand accounts of a press-gang raid, observations by Daniel Defoe, Charles Dickens, and Joshua Rowntree's vivid description of the 1914 bombardment by the German fleet. We visit Ann Bronte's grave at St Mary's and the magnificent pre-Raphaelite treasures in St Martin's-on-the-Hill. The place to be in the 1930s was the Tunny Club, visited by such celebrities as Baron Henri de Rothschild, John Wayne, the Asters, Errol Flynn, David Niven and Charles Laughton. Scarborough was the place where *Heroes Welcome Here* was set up and is still the headquarters for the movement which provides a welcome for Iraq and Afghanistan veterans.

Paul Chrystal
September 2014, York

# ABOUT THE AUTHOR

Paul Chrystal is author of more than thirty-five books published between 2010 and 2014 and a broadcaster. He has appeared regularly on BBC local radio and the BBC World Service and writes features for national newspapers. His books cover a wide range of subjects from local history to classical history. Recent titles include *Women in Ancient Rome*, 2013; *Chocolate: The British Chocolate Industry*, 2011; *Fry & Cadbury Through Time*, 2012; *York Then & Now*, 2010; *The History of Chocolate in York*, 2012; *The A-Z of York History*, 2013; *Lifeboat Stations of the North East*, 2012 (which includes Scarborough), and *The Rowntree Family, A Social History*, 2013 (which includes a chapter on Scarborough's Joshua Rowntree). Paul is married with three children and lives near York.

# ACKNOWLEDGEMENTS

Thanks to the following for help with and permissions to reproduce images: Karen Snowden at Scarborough Art Gallery; Angela Kale at Scarborough Library; Alan Avery at Blackthorn Press for permission to use the picture of Tostig, originally published in *Scarborough's Heroes, Rogues and Eccentrics* by Jack Binns; Bryan Berryman for permission to use images from his two books, *Scarborough As it Was* and *Vintage Scarborough*; the images of Scarborough after the 1941 blitz are courtesy of Scarborough Borough Council;

# CHAPTER 1
# HISTORY

## The Romans and their Signal Station

There is evidence of Stone Age settlers from around 8000 BC on the site of Scarborough; bronze age evidence from 500 BC has also been discovered. However, things really started to happen when the Romans came; in AD 370 they established a signal station here: a square tower in a square courtyard. The signal stations were designed to give protection against Anglo-Saxon pirates from southern Jutland and Frisia; torches were lit to alert the Roman army when raiders were sighted. They were the first of Scarborough's military fortifications: the most enduring, of course, being the castle.

### The Vikings Sack Scarborough

The Viking sagas make mention of Scarborough: in the *Kormakssaga*, *Flateyjarbo* Scarborough is Skarthborg and in the *Orkneyingasaga* it is Skarthabork. The *Kormakssaga* tells how two Viking brothers, Thorgils and Kormak, established a stronghold in AD 966 called Scarborough on the east coast. Thorgils was known by his nickname 'Hare Lip', or in Norse, 'Skarthi'. 'Hare-Lip' gave his name to Scarborough: Skarthi's Burgh, or Skarthi's Stronghold. In 1000 Christians built a chapel but in 1066 Hardrada, (Harald III, King of Norway) and Tostig Godwinson sack the town and destroy the chapel. They did such a good job that there was nothing left for *Domesday* to report in 1085. The upper illustration shows Tostig landing in Scarborough; the lower is the English Heritage Viking depicted at the entrance of the castle.

## Scarborough's Angevin castle

The castle was built around 1130 by William Le Gros, Earl of Albermarle, during the reign of King Henry I. Le Gros defeated the Scots at The Battle of the Standard near Northallerton in 1138. The castle was captured by Henry II (reigned 1133–1189) who rebuilt the keep around 1162 as part of his Angevin empire. He also granted the town charters in 1155 and 1163, allowing a market on the beach , and introducing rule by burgesses. Angevin derives from the countries ruled by the Angevin Plantagenet dynasty: roughly half of France, England, and part of Ireland. The view of the castle and St Mary's church by Ernest Haslehurst was originally published in *Our Beautiful Homeland* (1930) by George Benson. Ann Bronte's grave is in the modern photograph: she died in the town in 1849.

**Piers Gaveston and Scarborough Castle**

Scarborough Castle was one of the many gifts lavished on Piers Gaveston by the smitten Edward II (reigned 1284–1327). The castle was later besieged by the Barons Percy, Warenne, Clifford and Pembroke. Gaveston was taken prisoner, sent to Oxford and then to Warwick Castle to be executed. The card shows Volunteers leaving Scarborough Castle; it was posted in August 1905 two years before The Territorial and Reserve Forces Act 1907 which merged existing Volunteer and Yeomanry units into a new Territorial Force . The Boer War had shown that the regular Army could not fight a prolonged war without substantial support; nearly all the regular units had been deployed within four months, and all reserve manpower had been exhausted within a year.

### Scarborough Fair

In 1253 a royal charter gave rise to Scarborough Fair, a forty-five day long trade festival attended by merchants from all over Europe and the Byzantine Empire: 'The Burgesses and their heirs forever may have a yearly fair in the Borough, to continue from the Feast of the Assumption until the Feast of St Michael'. The fair lasted until the eighteenth century, and has been immortalised in the ballad *Scarborough Fair*. Scarborough and the castle changed hands seven times between Royalists and Parliamentarians during the Civil War and was subjected to two long sieges, reducing much of the town to ruins. The card is one of a series 37 printed in Saxony in 1895.

## Down t' Street

The photograph, taken around 1905, shows residents of Quay Street and Whitehead Hill in the old town—down t' street. It appeared in the *Scarborough Guide & Souvenir* published for the 1906 National Union of Teachers Conference. Considering the audience, and that Seebohm Rowntree's landmark *Poverty* had appeared just a few years earlier, the text is alarmingly naive: 'the quaint old alleys...should on no account be missed by delegates with antiquarian tastes, or by the amateur photographer in search of picturesque bits. In spite of evidence of poverty—for fishing is 'not what it was' ... there is much to interest'. Quay Street is built on reclaimed land; as the harbour inexorably silted up over time the quay was moved further out from its original site near where Quay Street is now. and was subjected to two long sieges, reducing much of the town to ruins.

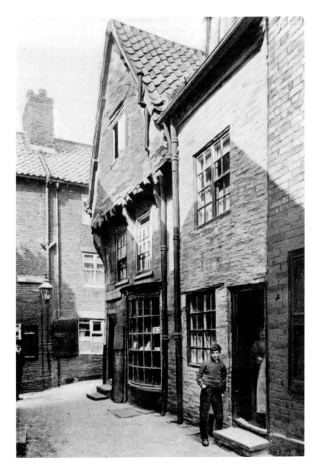

## William Morris

The picture shows more of the old town: Church Stairs Street, the church being St Mary the Virgin begun around 1200, reconstructed in the mid fifteenth century, then damaged during the siege of the castle in 1644; the central tower fell down in 1659. Another church, St Martin-on-the-Hill was built in 1862 and is a pre-Raphaelite paradise. William Morris' company did most of the stained glass and other decoration. The chancel is by William Morris and Philip Webb; the altar wall displays the *Adoration of the Magi* by Edward Burne-Jones; and the pulpit has ten painted panels by Dante Gabriel Rossetti, Ford Madox Brown and William Morris. The new photograph show two of the four R. Spencer-Stanhope angels on the organ casement.

**Richard III at Sandside**
Richard III was given the castle, the port
and the haven in 1473, when he was
Duke of Gloucester. He made the port
the base for his fleet, building a bulwark
to strengthen the harbour, improving
the town defences, and replacing
part of the Newborough moat with a
turreted stone wall. Richard apparently
stayed at the fourteenth-century
house on Sandside, pictured here.

### The Lighthouse: A Dim View

An early view of the harbour. Today the harbour comprises three piers enclosing an outer and inner harbour. The three piers are: the West Pier, completed 1325; the East Pier, from 1811; the Vincent Pier, completed in 1752. The outer harbour is used by leisure vessels and the inner harbour by fishing and passenger boats. The lighthouse is on the Vincent Pier. The first reference to it is in 1804 when a signal flag was displayed by day and a light by night from a coal brazier, later replaced by six tallow candles, hardly a shining beacon of safety; later this was augmented by a copper reflector behind the candles. In 1914 the lighthouse was damaged during the bombardment by the German navy, resulting in the dismantling of the tower. It was rebuilt in 1931.

**Boulevard Secondary School, Hull comes to Scarborough**

At the beginning of the Second World War pupils and staff were evacuated from the Boulevard Secondary School (later Kingston High School) in Hull. Their destination was the Astoria Hotel where they were to spend the next few years in relative safety. This and the following photograph were originally published in John D. Hicks' *A Hull School in Wartime* published by Highgate Publications; the photos were taken by Messrs Walker of Scarborough. The 120 or so girls and teachers here were just a few of the 16,000 evacuees from Hull and the 8,500 from West Hartlepool and Hartlepool. The modern picture shows a 1914 Vickers Pattern 13 pdr gun raised 100 feet from the sea bed by Scarborough Sub Aqua Club and local fishermen in 1982. It was originally on the *SS Hornsund*—a British cargo ship—which was sunk by German torpedo in 1917, two and a half miles off Scarborough.

## Evacuation Rations

On arrival every child was given a carrier bag packed by staff from W. Rowntree & Sons, Marshall & Snelgrove, Dennis the Printers and Woolworths. The bags contained one tin of corned beef, a tin each of unsweetened and sweetened milk, 1 lb of biscuits; ¼ lb of chocolate or two chocolate crisps. A number of the evacuees were infested with lice and fleas; a cleansing centre was established in the Junior Instruction Centre in St Sepulchre Street. Here they were washed, deloused and re-clothed. By November 3,696 evacuees had returned home, and by April 1940 6,000 had left. The Diving Belle is resplendent in the newer photograph—a symbol of the town's position as first seaside resort and its recent regeneration.

# Chapter 2
# Scarborough and The Sea

**Scotch fisher lasses at work**

This card, posted in 1910 shows 'Scotch fisher lasses at work' and barrelmen dealing with a catch. For one month every year the fisher women would descend on Scarborough, often with their children, to process the herring catches. The children would steal any that escaped the barrels and go round the town selling them. In September they would all pack up and move on to the next port as the herring shoals moved down the coast. The new picture shows a crab catch being processed today.

**Scotch fisher lasses not at work**
A slack period in between catches for the fisher lasses. They continued to come to Scarborough and other ports until the 1960s. The photograph was originally published in *101 Views of Scarborough and District* published in 1890. The modern picture shows the modern face of the fish industry in Scarborough inside the Ocean's Pantry on the West Pier, run, appropriately, by Bob Scarborough.

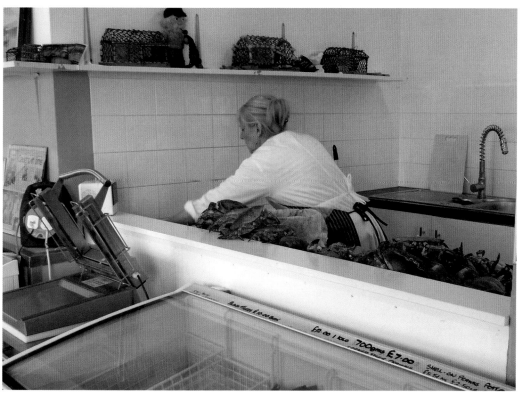

FISHING FLEET. SCARBOROUGH.

## Fishing at Scarborough

Scarborough fishing enjoyed a boom between 1830 and 1840; the 'Silver Pit' was discovered, quite by accident, in 1835 when a trawler disoriented in a storm off Dogger Bank found its nets full of sole. When the railways came in 1845 there was another boom as the York–Scarborough railway opened access to markets in York and further afield—transportation of catches had always been a problem for the Scarborough fishing industry.

### U-57 and the Sinking of the Fishing Fleet

On 25 September 1916 a German U-boat (U-57) single-handedly sank eleven Scarborough trawlers in one night; *The Mercury* reported that, 'The crews were landed at other ports, Shields and Hartlepool, and until their safety was notified there was great anxiety'. One, *The Ben Hope*, escaped leaving the Scarborough fleet with four boats. In 1920 three more were sank when they hit unexploded mines. Old catch and new catch in the pictures: a whole hake takes pride of place in The Ocean's Pantry.

### When the Boat Comes In

A description of the Scarborough fishing industry from *Theakston's Hand-Book for Strangers in Scarboro* published in 1862: 'When the smaller sized herring boats, or cobles, come to Scarborough to sell their fish, they generally lie on the western sands: and the appearance they sometimes present, reminds one of a large gipsy encampment, with the smoke curling up from behind the large outspread sail or net; and as many of them belong to the neighbouring smaller ports, the little boat becomes the home for the time of the sturdy fisherman... his fire burns as brightly, his kettle sings as cheerily, and his pan hisses away as merrily, as they would do in yonder hotel; and he is withal as satisfied with his frugal meal, for which the labours of the early morning have given him so true an appetite, as he who, lazily rising at noon, breakfasts from the dainties of a dozen dishes.' The card was posted in 1903 and shows the busy fish market.

### Tunny Fishing and Zane Grey

In 1929 blue fin tuna were 'discovered' in the North Sea prompting a minor industry more akin to big game hunting than fishing, as we know it. In 1930 a 735 lb tunny was caught off Scarborough by a Fred Taylor just 23 lb below Zane Grey's world record Nova Scotia 758 lb fish. August 1932 saw a seven hour ten minute duel between a sixteen feet tuna and Harold Hardy of Cloughton Hall; he was 'within an ace of hauling it aboard when, in its dying struggle the fish snapped the line and escaped'.

**The Fashionable British Tunny Club**
The British Tunny Club was formed in Scarborough in 1933 and is now a fish and chip restaurant, The Tunny Club at 1 Eastgate. The tunnies attracted visitors from all over Europe: in 1934 Baron Henri de Rothschild arrived in his 1,000 ton yacht Eros. John Wayne, The Asters, Errol Flynn, David Niven and Charles Laughton are all alleged to have visited. In 1954 the last tunny fish was caught off the Scarborough coast—a bad sign for the herring industry as tuna typically fed on the shoals of migrating herrings.

THE HARBOUR SCARBOROUGH.

## Dickens and Scarborough

In his *Household Words* published in 1851 Charles Dickens describes the graveyard of St Mary's: 'But for abundant and overwhelming evidences of the dangerous life of sea-faring men, a churchyard of a town like Scarborough is the place. There the old Church of St Mary... exhibits as densely crowded a scene of tombstones as any graveyard of the metropolis itself... Yet still how many stones are mere memorials of those whose bones are scattered over the wide earth, and throng the deepest depths of the sea, We can only indicate a few of the multitude who have perished in every imaginable region, and have mementos here. William Allen, drowned at Charente, Nov. 1829, aged thirteen years; sad Joseph Allan, son of the above (sic), drowned by the overturning of a life-boat, Feb. 17th, 1836, aged thirteen years.' The images show fishermen and anglers at work in the 1910s, and on a foggy day in March 2013.

SCARBOROUGH-LAUNCH OF THE LIFEBOAT

### Black-Eyed Susan and The Glastry

The schooner *Glastry* was one of the many ships in trouble off Scarborough during the great storm of 27 to 30 October 1880; the lifeboat on service was the *Lady Leigh*. The *Scarborough Mercury* reported: 'As soon as daylight appeared, crowds of people thronged the cliffs, gasping with anxious eyes across the wild expanse of water, which for miles around was foaming and seething with terrible fury'. Before ending up on the beach the *Glastry* collided with the brig *Lily*; other vessels in distress were the *Mary*, the *Jeune Adolphi* and the *Black Eyed Susan*. The crew of the *Glastry* left the ship before it broke free and drifted off again.

## Herbert Joy II and Queen Mary

13 November 1901 saw a storm raging off Scarborough; the *Edward and Lucille* (1900–1902) went to the aid of the stricken brigantine Boxer en route to Hartlepool with a cargo of chalk; beached in South Bay its eight man crew were successfully taken off and the wreck was sold off for £8. Scarborough's Lifeboat station, established in 1801, is the third oldest in the United Kingdom after Sunderland and Montrose. Thomas Hinderwell, the Scarborough historian, was the impetus for the establishment of a lifeboat here. In 1799 he told of an heroic rescue involving four Scarborough fishermen who rowed in an open coble from Scarborough to a ship in distress off Filey, and of other acts of bravery in other rescues. This led to his campaign for a lifeboat in 1800. The card shows the Herbert Joy II launched on 5 August 1931 by Queen Mary. Today's lifeboat is the *Fanny Victoria Wilkinson and Francis Stubbs*.

*The Fortunes of War*
One of the wonderful sand sculptures that appeared on Scarborough's beaches. This one was called *The Fortunes of War*; the card was posted in 1918.

## Storm Damage

Storm damage to the spa wall on a card painted by Henry Wanless and posted in 1908. The angry sea continues to plague Scarborough to this day despite millions of pounds spent on sea defences. Famously, in June 1993 part of the Holbeck Hall Hotel and its gardens fell into the sea: altogether 27,000 m² of mud slipped, finally protruding 100 metres further into the sea than the original coastline. The slip had nothing to do with the sea, however: it was caused by soil creep which itself was caused by a period of heavy rain.

### Tindall's Yard

Two interesting pictures taken from exactly the same spot, Castle Dykes, some thirty years apart. In the top picture Scarborough's ship-building industry is thriving in Tindall's Yard with possibly the last boat built there, *The Clyde*, registered in 1863. By the time the second picture was taken around 1890 this has all gone and all that remains is a small fishing industry.

# Chapter 3
# Scarborough the Spa

DICKY DICKINSON,
Governour of Scarborough Spaw.

*SAMOS unenvy'd boasts her Æsop gone*
*And FRANCE may glory in her late Scarron*
*While ENGLAND has a Living Dickinson.*

Sold by C. Want & R. Chandler near Temple Bar; & at their shop in Scarborough

**Thomasin Farrer Discovers the Waters**
Scarborough's spa potential was discovered by a Mrs Thomasin Farrer in the late 1620s who found spring water bubbling out of the Driple Cotes cliffs in the south of the town. The waters stained the rocks a reddish brown and tasted bitter. Word spread rapidly regarding the putative medicinal qualities of the waters. According to Mrs Farrer, the waters '*did both loose the belly, and also amend the stomach, and cure some distempers*'. The image on page 31 is from a card showing the spaw from a lithograph by J. Stubbs in 1827. The images here are of the first Governor of the Spaw, Dicky Dickinson; see page 34.

## The Crackfart of Scarborough Spaw

In 1691 the corporation introduced a charge of 1 shilling per gallon and built a cistern in 1698. A Dr Whittie published *Scarborough Spa* in 1660 which promoted the waters' healthy qualities. Wittie, though, did not have it all his own way: competition came from Dr William Simpson's *Hydrologia Chymica* which Wittie described as being *'fit only for bum-fother'*; a Geordie, George Tunstall, called Wittie *'the crackfart of Scarborough Spaw'*. The success of the spa led to Scarborough becoming Britain's first seaside resort. Here are just a few of the activities available to the fashionable spa-goer.

### Dicky Dickinson: *'one of the most deformed pieces of mortality'*

Scarborough waters were also reputedly successful in curing *'hypochondriachal wind'*, rapid voiding of worms and banishing *'a scorbutick elephantiasis'* (a type of scurvy). The first Governor of the Spa was the eccentric, deformed, ex-shoe-shiner Dicky Dickinson, described variously as *'perhaps the most singular deformity in the king's dominions'* and *'one of the most deformed pieces of mortality'*. Others compared him with the letter 'z': unable to stand up straight and perpetually in a posture *'fit to shite'*. But his scathing wit made him something of a celebrity nationwide and added to the attraction of Scarborough spa; this, combined with notable business acumen, made him extremely wealthy.

### The Spaw and The Cliff Bridge Company

Profits from the spaw paid for a new house of correction, workhouse and prison. In the early 1700s a spa house was built to sell the waters to increasing numbers of visitors; a wooden wharf designed to offer protection from the sea was washed away in 1735. Two years later a cliff fall destroyed the wells and the spa house. In the 1820s the The Cliff Bridge Company leased the spa from the Corporation and in 1827 erected an iron footbridge enabling access to the Spa from St Nicholas Cliff; they also built a 'gothic' saloon in 1839 which included a concert hall for 500 people, gardens, a promenade and an outside area for orchestras. But all this was far too small to accommodate the hordes of visitors and Sir Joseph Paxton, famous for his work at Chatsworth and Crystal Palace, built additional facilities increasing the capacity to 2,000 in 1848. The Italianate Royal Northern Sea Bathing Infirmary, built in the 1850s, is depicted on the card with nurses and patients on the balcony around 1905. It later became St Thomas's Hospital.

**Scarborough Spaw: '*horrid*', and '*as dismal as a funeral*'**

Scarborough had been slow to capitalise on its precious waters: in 1697 Celia Fiennes found a '*very pretty seaport town*' with no spa facilities; in 1732 the Duchess of Marlborough thought it '*horrid*', the company '*as dismal as a funeral*', and dirty compared with Bath or Tunbridge Wells while the food was worse than in Hanover. A fire gutted the pavilion in 1877 and in 1879 a new pavilion emerged, opened by the Lord Mayor of London. See pages 34 and 37.

**Fireworks at the Spaw**
The *Illustrated London News* recorded the event in its issue of 11 August 1880. The pictures show the reception at the Royal Hotel, the actual opening ceremony and the firework display. Jools Holland and Ruby Turner provide the entertainment nowadays.

**The Spaw Galvanised**
Dr Robert Wittie's *Scarbrough Spaw* which described the health-giving qualities of the spa waters: good for '*frequent fluxes of the belly*'. This not only served to attract thousands of visitors but it also spawned a minor industry of somewhat dubious pharmaceutical and other therapies. Galvanism (electrophysiology) is the contraction of a muscle that is stimulated by an electric current: it is named after Luigi Galvani who was investigating the effect of electricity on dissected animals in the 1780s when his scalpel touched a frog, making the muscles in the frog's leg twitch. Galvani called it animal electricity; Mary Shelley's Frankenstein was brought to life through galvanism.

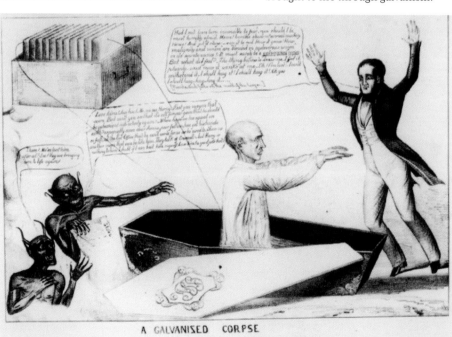

A GALVANISED CORPSE

# Chapter 4
# Scarborough the Resort

**The First Seaside Resort**

The spa paved the way for Scarborough to become a resort in the fullest sense of the word. The entertainment required to keep the spa-goers busy and amused elided almost seamlessly into what was required of a seaside resort in the nineteenth century. The card here shows the fashionable visitors to the town on the South Cliff in a painting by H. B. Carter from around 1850. The modern picture shows the balconies on Esplanade apartments.

**Fashionable Scarborough**

These fashionable ladies were published in *The Graphic* in 1870. Uncle Joe wrote the post card to a Miss Ivy in 1911; with Aunty Jane he '*is watching the little girls play on the Sands some as got their Shoes and Stocking of and are Paddling in the sea. We are having a good time wishing you was here*'. The Grand Hotel opened in 1867 and, at the time was 'the largest and handsomest in Europe'. The picture on page 42 shows the Grand Hotel horse carriage sheds and the site, under the bridge, of the Indo-Moorish Scarborough Aquarium, which opened in 1877. It covered two and a quarter acres, was lit by 1,600 gas jets, its decoration based on Hindu temples; it boasted a Japanese theatre and villages. Scarborough Council ran the buildings as *Galaland* between 1925 and 1966, but it was demolished soon after.

THE BOYS ARE RATHER CHEEKY

### Scarborough and the Press Gang

Scarborough was not always genteel fashionability 'though; these extracts from Baker's *History of Scarborough* show how the press gang worked locally in the seventeenth century: Richard Sellars says, '*I was pressed between Scarbrough piers in the time of the last two engagements between the Dutch and English in the year 1665, and refusing to go on board the ketch, they beat me sore on the sands and then hoisted me in with a tackle, so that I fell backward into a tub and was maimed... then the boatswain beat me sore. The captain sent for me on the quarter-deck, and asked why I refused to fight for the king, and why I declined to eat of his victuals. So I told him I was afraid to offend God, therefore I could not fight with carnal weapons. Then he fell upon me and beat me*'. The new picture shows the Mount Hotel through the Spa Bridge.

CHURCH PARADE, SOUTH CLIFF, SCARBOROUGH.

*'Take the Quakerly dog away'*
A busy Esplanade with the ritual Church Parade in 1908. Sellers goes on: *'Then said the captain, 'He is a Quaker and I will beat his brains out,' and calling for the boatswain bade him 'take the Quakerly dog away and put him to the capstan.' On the third day after came the admiral, Sir Edward Spragge... the boatswain was commanded to put me in irons... and to call a council of war, which was done...*

## *Hispaniola*, pirate ship

*... the next morning being come, on which I had to be executed about eight o'clock, the rope being reeved upon the mizen yard-arm, and the boy ready to turn me off; the captains of the other ships having come on board, I was thereupon called to come to be executed, so I stepped on board the gunwale to go forward to the rope. The commander bid me stop there if I had anything to say. Then he added 'silence, all men,' and proclaimed the Quaker was a free man as any on board the ship. So the men heaved up their hats and with a loud voice cried 'God bless Sir Edward, he is a merciful man'.* The photographs show a crewman, the captain, being assisted aboard his boat, the pirate ship *Hispaniola*, and the *Hispaniola* setting sail.

**Scarborough Pubs**
As with any market town and port there is a plethora of pubs in Scarborough. Here is a small sample of those with more attractive signs and symbols.

45

**Castle Hill from the Harbour**
Two views of Castle Hill about fifty years apart clearly show the development of the harbour and town between 1910 and 1960.

### The Largest Pool in Europe

When it was built in 1915, Scarborough's South Bay salt-water bathing pool was the largest outdoor pool in Europe: 330 feet long and 167 feet wide. The card shows it in 1922. It was originally designed and built not just to be a bathing pool, but also to act as a cushioning wave barrier. After a new pool, the *Atlantis*, was built in the North Bay this closed in 1988 and was demolished and landscaped over in 2003.

47

### All the Fun of the Beach

Pierrots (the Catlins), bathing machines, Punch & Judy, horses in the lower picture from around 1900. *Catlin's Favourite Pierrots* were a frequent feature around 1905 on the South Shore. The earliest beach entertainers were the Home Minstrels in the 1880s and 1890s; their number included David Hunter who played cricket for Yorkshire. Will Catlin shrewdly built up a loyal (female) following by presenting his troupe as eligible bachelors, forbidding them to be seen arm in arm with women, even though some of the pierrots were married. The older image was drawn by John Leech and published in the *Illustrated London News* on 26 September 1857.

## The Country's First Cliff Tramway

This was one of five cliff tramways built in Scarborough; three on South Bay and two on North Bay. The first on the South Bay was the first in the country opened in 1875 linking the esplanade with the Spa. Another below Queen's Parade only lasted from 1878 to 1887. The North Bay lift here was opened in 1930 and closed in 1996. The modern photograph shows the tramway at the Spa in operation today.

**Scarborough's Five Ladies**

*The White Lady* in 1927, the first of Thomas Round's fleet of five ladies: *Yorkshire Lady*, *White Lady II*, *Royal Lady* and *New Royal Lady* were the others. The *Coronia* (see page 5) = *HMS Watchfull*, and the *Regal Lady* (or *Oulton Bell*) arrived after the Second World War, the *Regal Lady* having seen service at Dunkirk in 1940.

**Holiday Life in Scarborough**

This page from an 1881 edition of *The Graphic* neatly encapsulates a holiday in Scarborough: *1. Unloading fish; 2. Spa darlings; 3. Children on the shore; 4. Children on the prom; 5. Ladies going to the Bath; 6. Starting under difficulties; 7. At Dinner; 8. On the harbour pier.*

### The Crown

The Crown Hotel opened in 1845 and was the first hotel on the South Cliff; it was designed with a distinct Graeco-Roman theme. The first of many advertisements in *The Times* read as follows: *J. F. SHARPIN respectfully informs the Nobility and Gentry that he has entered upon the above new anti-extensive Establishment, which he is having fitted up in a superior manner with entirely new furniture, and purposes being ready for the reception of Visitors on the 10th of June next...The number of apartments exceeds 120, consisting of various suites of dining, sitting, and lodging rooms, including a magnificent Drawing room, sixty feet long... Hot, Cold, and Shower Baths have been fitted on the most approved plan, and can be had on the shortest notice, are easy of access and will be available also to the Visitors of the adjoining neighbourhood. The Stabling is adapted for 60 horses, the lock-up houses for 40 carriages, and the minor accommodations of the court-yard are in equal ratio.*

**The Foreshore and Men in Jackets**

The Foreshore Road pictured on a card from Thomas Nelson & Sons in the late nineteenth century, more famous for their book publishing. The 'new' card shows the same scene in 1957, sent from Maude to Eliza in Foul Anchor, near Wisbech. Note the men wearing their jackets.

**A Band of Egyptians**

The thirteen storey Grand Hotel rises imposingly in the background in this 1930s card (see page 42). The lower picture shows one of the posters outside the Tunny Club. Scarborough, as anywhere else, is not without its eccentrics: in 1579 Phillip and Katherine Bastian were indicted for leaving Scarborough to join a band of Egyptians; Timothy Fish bought a pew in St Mary's church in 1710 measuring a truly capacious eight feet by five feet.

SCARBOROUGH

1930 BOOKLET FREE FROM TOWN HALL OR ANY L·N·E·R AGENCY

An Obsession with Chairs

The harbour meant as much fun as the beach to these children. In 1724 Phatuel Ford's Newborough mansion contained twenty-one red leather chairs, seven other leather chairs of assorted colours, eighteen cane chairs, and an arm chair. In 1875 an attacking harpooner leaped on the back of a whale; his harpoon failed. John Wrench was licensed by the Scarborough bailiffs in 1697 as a badger.

### Valley Bridge

Valley Bridge in Ramsdale Valley from Cliff Bridge in 1889. Valley Bridge went up in 1865 but it always had an air of second-handedness about it. It was actually salvaged from the River Ouse in York after it collapsed and was shipped here to Scarborough. It was to be York's first bridge over the Ouse (Lendal Bridge) and was designed by the aptly-named William Dredge. Unfortunately, this bridge collapsed during construction killing five men; the remnants of Dredge's bridge were dredged up from the river and sold to Scarborough Council. A new Valley Bridge opened in 1928. The new photograph shows the Spa footbridge.

### The First Bathing Machines

Scarborough pioneered bathing machines for women, who went into the sea fully clothed assisted by servant women, from horse drawn sheds on wheels. Men just swam naked. One visitor complained of the 'discreditable jumbling together of the sexes and the absence of proper hoods on the bathing machines'. The Corporation imposed strict rules regarding bathing areas, distances to be kept between men and women and bathing clothes to be worn, from 7 a.m. to 9 p.m. *The Graphic* said in 1871 that it was absurd that a house, a horse and an attendant were needed to get a woman into the sea. A Leeds visitor said '*mixed bathing is the halfway house to mixed sleeping and might be a plank on the river leading to the Niagara of eternal damnation*'.

Bathing Machines.

**Punchinello and ... Joan**

The Punch and Judy show derives from the sixteenth-century Italian *commedia dell'arte*. Punch comes from the character of Neapolitan Pulcinella, which became *Punchinello*: a manifestation of the Lord of Misrule and Trickster figures. Punch's wife was originally called Joan. Mr Punch made his debut in England on 9 May 1662, which is now regarded as Punch's birthday in the UK. Samuel Pepys watched a marionette show featuring an early version of Punch in Covent Garden.

# CHAPTER 5
# BUSINESS
# SCARBOROUGH

VIEW FROM RESTAURANT
W·ROWNTREE & SONS·

The Well-known Store .
on the Yorkshire Coast .

33-39, Westborough,
**Scarborough.** .

### The Rowntrees

W. Rowntree was one of the town's premier stores. The elder Joseph Rowntree (1801–1859) was born in Carr Street and later worked in his father's grocery business. When he was twenty-one he moved to York and set up himself as a grocer in Pavement. It was his second son, Joseph (born in 1836) who, having worked in Pavement for a number of years went on to develop Rowntree's, the world famous chocolate company. Joseph's nephew, Joshua, was born in 1844 in Princess Street, Scarborough and went on to become a lawyer and the town's MP. The fantastic mural on page 59 can be seen in the vaults at the Market Hall.

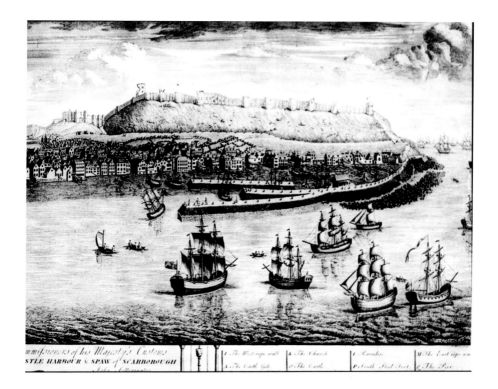

**John Setterington's Scarborough Map**

John Setterington's Scarborough showing the town in 1735 with its maritime trade and fishing industry. The engraving also features the spa and the first known depiction of bathing machines, indicating the town's nascent tourist industry.

**Scarborough Market Hall**

Opened in 1853 the market hall is 151 feet long, 111 feet wide and 43 feet high. It was the culmination of a long history of markets in the town: the Saturday market was in Princess Street (formerly Nether Westgate) where there are still the remains of the Old Market Cross, or Butter Cross, at Low Conduit Street. Thursday Market was in Newborough Street selling pots, glass, and earthenware; the apple market was held in King Street, the cattle market in Queen Street, the pig market in Tanner Street, and the meat market in St Helen's Square in the Old Shambles; these butchers stalls, slaughterhouses, tallow and bone yards, were demolished to make way for the 1853 building.

**Whiter than Driven Snow**

A scene inside the Snowdrift Laundry. The laundry was built on the site of a tannery and a well. The newer picture shows one of the shops in the Market Vaults: this is Icke Oyate—First Nation—an amazing collection of native Indian and 'wild west' artefacts, memorabilia and paraphernalia— probably one of the best in Europe.

### Three Mariners Inn

One of Scarborough's many pubs—the *Three Mariners Inn* as painted by Marjorie Bates RA (1882–1962). The pub is one of Scarborough's oldest, dating back to the 1300s. It is certainly one of the most haunted—by a headless woman, who warns fishermen of impending doom and disaster. The pub is now a museum charting the history of smuggling in the area; it was linked to the shore by a series of caves and tunnels and features secret cupboards, false floors and hidden rooms. There is even a very small window used as a look out down Quay Street. Over the years the *Three Mariners* has revealed some of its secret past: a concealed room has been discovered there which contained a keg of gunpowder; a small boy broke through some plaster one day to find himself trapped in a small cupboard—only his cries revealed his whereabouts.

Newborough

Fashionable shopping in Newborough in the 1890s, with Boots in the background. Boots was founded in 1849, by John Boot; he died in 1860; his son, Jesse Boot, aged ten , started helping his mother run the family's herbal medicine shop in Nottingham, which became Boot and Co Ltd in 1883, then Boots Pure Drug Company Ltd in 1888. In the 1960s Boots developed ibuprofen. The new picture shows the fine clock at the junction of Newborough and Westborough.

65

### 'Heroes Welcome Here' 1900 and 2013

Scarborough has a long history of honouring and welcoming the country's servicemen and war heroes, as this early 1900s Sandside grocer shop poster shows. A century later in 2008 a hand-drawn poster stating *'Heroes Welcome Here'* was displayed in the Golden Grid Fish Restaurant, thus establishing Scarborough as the first Heroes Welcome town for servicemen past and present who have served in Iraq and Afghanistan. The website takes up the story: *'From this gesture has evolved a national network of Heroes Welcome Towns, Cities and Counties. Heroes Welcome UK is free to join and is designed to encourage British communities to demonstrate their open support to members of the Armed Forces. Businesses are invited to display a Heroes Welcome sticker indicating a special welcome to service personnel'*. Heroes Welcome UK is run from Scarborough: *www.heroeswelcome.org/*

**Scarborough's Shipping Industry**
These cards evoke the maritime character of Scarborough. All manner of boats are routinely stranded at low tide; before the First World War over 300 fishing boats worked out of Scarborough.

"Harbour Life".
THE LIGHTHOUSE, SCARBOROUGH.

Scottish Fisher Girls, Scarborough

### The Herring Industry

The annual herring season was important business for Scarborough. Here the immigrant workers (from Scotland) in the early 1900s provide something of a fascination for the well-heeled visitors to the resort. Scarborough was the fifth largest herring port in the country; the best girls could gut, clean, grade and sort fifty herrings every minute. Once processed the herrings were stored in the barrels shown here, and packed with ice and salt. Some of the haul was exported to Russia.

### George Rowntree and the Bombardment

Scarborough trade was not immune from the 1914 bombardment; this grocer's in Prospect Street was hit; the owner's wife was killed in the doorway helping casualties. The modern picture shows a modern, inventive, take on an old craft. This is how George Rowntree, in his Reminiscences, graphically described the raid:

*'I looked through the window, and to my horror saw a shell strike Mr. Turner's house, 'Dunollie,' just below us. Then another terrific explosion, and a mass of smoke and debris rose in the air... Then came the heaviest firing; the noise was terrific. We could hear the swish, swish of the shells as they came over us and burst on Oliver's Mount. Some burst amongst the trees; four fell in the field on our north. Mountside was struck with three shells; Queen Margaret's Hall was badly shelled; several houses below us, Netherbank, Saxifield, Shortlands, were all badly damaged...*

### The Bombardment Goes On...

Paddling in front of the Spa in 1928. George Rowntree continues... *No district in Scarborough escaped. About 300 houses were struck, and the Coastguard considered that anywhere up to 500 shells were fired... Many have left their homes; people fled from the town along the York Road and the trains were filled with rich and poor... Two ladies left their home on the South Cliff with their long hair down their backs, and in their hurry left their false teeth on the breakfast table. One man put his Christmas Cake under his arm; a woman who did not like to leave her best silk dress for the Germans quickly put it on'.* Later in the war, in September 1917, a lone U-Boat shelled the town killing three people.

**Odeon Corner**

This 1931 photograph shows the busy junction opposite the railway station. The plethora of buses and trolleybuses can be explained by the fact that in September 1931 they had replaced the trams. Today the Odeon is occupied by the Stephen Joseph Theatre, run by Alan Ayckbourn and named after the innovative Stephen Joseph who developed the theatre in the round in the Britain.

## Life and Death in the Workhouse

When it all went wrong this is where, more often than not, you ended up. This is the new workhouse in Dean Street as depicted in an 1860 edition of the *Illustrated London News*. The first Scarborough workhouse opened in 1728, and was in Waterhouse Lane. Rules were strict with the sexes segregated and profanity, indecency and drunkenness prohibited. Old men 'that are past work' were allowed out on Tuesdays and Friday afternoons, and all inmates on Saturday from four until six in the evening. Some sold bread to buy snuff and tea. A fever ward was built in 1847; men laboured at stone-breaking while women washed, cleaned, cooked and repaired clothes. The new 1859 workhouse cost £12,000 and accommodated up to 400 inmates; the infirmary is at the rear. It later became Scarborough Public Assistance Institution; in 1936 a mental ward was opened. In 1940 the vagrants' wards were closed and the building became St Mary's Hospital in 1948, closing around 2000. The new picture is of Wilson's Mariners' Homes founded in 1894 as 'almshouses for poor aged persons of good character being shipowners (having been nautical people), shipmates, mates, seagoing carpenters or mariners and their wives or widows or unmarried daughters being not less than 50 years of age who have resided in the Borough of Scarborough for not less than ten years'.

# Chapter 6
# Scarborough Disasters

## The German Bombardment

In the early morning of 16 December 1914 Scarborough was to be one of four north east coastal towns bombarded by the German fleet. In the space of forty minutes about 1,000 shells were first unleashed on Hartlepool and West Hartlepool from three German heavy cruisers *Blücher*, *Seydlitz* and *Moltke*, killing sixty-three civilians and nine soldiers in Hartlepool and fifty-six civilians in West Hartlepool; 400 or so civilians were injured and much housing stock was damaged or destroyed. The raid on the Hartlepools was followed by similar assaults on Scarborough and Whitby in which eighteen and three people were killed respectively.

MINE SWEEPER Nº58. DAMAGED BY GERMAN MINES OFF SCARBOROUGH.

### The *Derfflinger* and *von der Tann* Come to Town

The Royal Navy had received advance warning of the raid from the naval intelligence unit (the 'Room 40' group) and Admiral Warrender was despatched with six battleships, four battle cruisers, four heavy cruisers, six light cruisers and eight submarines to intercept the German raiding force. Just before the attack on Hartlepool, Warrender spotted the Germans but astonishingly mistook them for an insignificant raiding party. Off Scarborough the *Derfflinger* and *von der Tann* opened fire on the coastguard station and the barracks before shelling the castle and the Grand Hotel, believing it to be a gun battery. As they passed Whitby they fired fifty rounds at the signal station town and Abbey. The attack on the east coast caused outrage in Britain: partly because the Navy failed to intercept the Germans, but also because Whitby and Scarborough, unlike Hartlepool, were undefended, open towns. *Scarborough Maritime Heritage Centre News* points out in its March 2013 edition that all histories of the bombardment *claim that the Germans fired 'around 500 shells' into the town, whereas the official German Naval Archives show that 333 'large calibre' (11 inch and 12 inch shells) and 443 'medium calibre' shells were fired—a total of 776.*

GERMAN RAID, DEC. 16ᵗʰ 1914. INTERIOR OF HOUSE.

**The Boyes Blaze**
All that remained of the remnant warehouse on Queen Street belonging to William Boyes on 26 February 1915. The badly damaged Queen Street Chapel is in the background. The Boyes store in York had been destroyed by fire in 1910.

## The End of the Pier

All that remained of the North Promenade Pier after the storm on 8 January 1905. It was designed by Eugenius Birch the creator of Brighton's pier and opened on 5 July 1869. Entrance charges were 1d a day and 6d for a weekly ticket. The pier was 1,000 feet long and twenty-three feet wide, with seating on both sides. It was never a financial success. New owners in 1880 added a pavilion and shops, but to no avail. It was sold again in 1904 then finally destroyed in a storm in 1905.

**Storm Damage**
More storm damage, this time March 1905 outside the Spa showing a wrecked sea wall. The new picture shows Scarborough sea defences today.

## Civic Vandalism and the Bars

More of a tragedy really than a disaster, but a disaster all the same—the fate of Scarborough's bars is as bad an example of civic hooliganism and vandalism as you are likely to find. Newborough Bar was demolished for the specious purposes of making traffic improvements. The Gothic Revival Westborough had been built in 1850 and destroyed in 1890. Newborough, pictured here and the main gateway into the town , was in the same style, built in 1843; its predecessor dated from the mid-twelfth century and is depicted here around 1530. There was originally a ditch in front of a gate, crossed by a drawbridge. Newborough housed the town prison from the thirteenth to the nineteenth century: *'the arch of misery'*.

79

### The Scarborough Blitz

On 26 June 1940 hostile Germans were back. A lone bomber dropped nine bombs and incendiaries along the road at Burniston damaging five cottages. In October another lone bomber dropped a parachute mine on Potter Lane and Short's Gardens (now Castle Gardens) creating a six feet wide and thirty feet deep crater, damaging over 500 houses, seventy-one of which had to be written off. Two adults and two children—evacuees were killed but the death toll would have been much higher had not many of the residents been out at a Spitfire dance and whist drive at the Olympia Ballroom. The photographs on this and the next two pages were provided courtesy of Scarborough Borough Council and show damage after the October 1940 raid and Castle Gardens after a raid on 18 March 1941.

Dennis Destroyed

Scarborough suffered over twenty raids, the worst of which was the 18 March 1941 blitz in which ninety-eight bombers dropped over 1,000 incendiaries and fifty-five high explosive bombs and mines, killing twenty-eight people and destroying or damaging 1,378 buildings. Printers and publishers of a number of postcards used in this book, E. T. W. Dennis & Sons, in Melrose Street was destroyed.

### Margaret Willis, Guide Extraordinaire

The George Medal was awarded to Capt. Hugh Davidson Miller MD of the Royal Army Medical Corps who displayed 'conspicuous courage' in attending to casualties during the raid. He had crawled under the wreckage of No. 1 Queens Terrace which had received a direct hit with high explosive bombs and a delayed action bomb. The home of Margaret Willis (later Shaw) at 63 Commercial Street was destroyed by a parachute mine; Margaret comforted her family under the stairs for a full nine hours before they were rescued. She was awarded the Gilt Cross of the Girl Guides Association; her little sister was killed and both her parents lost a leg.

# CHAPTER 7
# SCARBOROUGH ENTERTAINMENT

Annual Charity Football Match & Tug-of-war Contest.

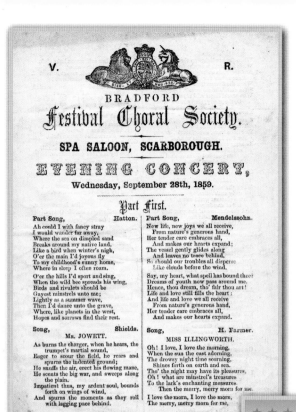

Bradford Choral Society Comes to Town
The pictures on page 83 show the Coronation Minstrels and, lower, Scarborough's fisherman and firemen about to compete in the annual football match and tug-of-war on Boxing Day 1907. The entertainment for 28September 1859 is shown in this Spa Saloon programme: an evening concert of songs by the Bradford Choral Society. Modern fare in the modern picture.

## The Pageants

The 1912 pageant took place in July in Castle Yard. It was described in Wonderful Britain by F. A. Mackenzie in 1920 as follows: 'a series of dramatic episodes, full of life and colour, was given especially associated with the sea life of the coast people from the days of the Iberians and Gaels and so through the centuries to the time of the press gang and the smugglers'.

THE BELLE of the
SCARBOROUGH PAGEANT

*Winter*

'Winter' at the pageant. The card was posted on 18 August by Ada to Margaret in Hackness; she had had a 'jolly time' at Scalby Show and has had her 'teeth stopped this week'(?). A production of John Godber's *Muddy Cows* is advertised in the newer photograph.

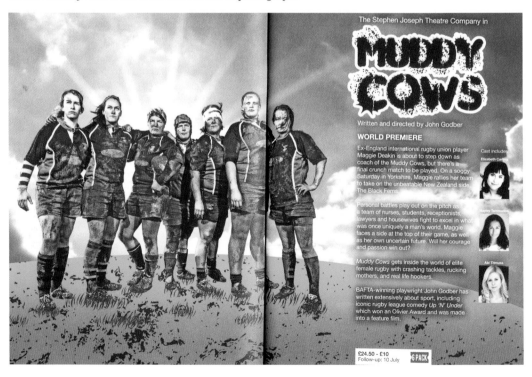

OPEN AIR THEATRE, SCARBOROUGH. — HIAWATHA — Spring Ballet. 2.

*Hiawatha*

A production of *Hiawatha* at the Open Air Theatre in 1971 which featured native American Indians in canoes paddling to the stage. Scarborough's Open Air Theatre was the largest in Europe opening in 1932 with *Merrie England*. The football pitch sized stage was on an island in the middle of a lake with seating for 5,876. By 1952 it had attracted 1.5 million people with casts of up to 200; in the eleven week summer season there were two performances a week. The last concert to be held at the Open Air Theatre before its closure in 1986 was, appropriately, James Last and His Orchestra.

SCARBOROUGH OPEN AIR THEATRE

SEASON 1938 : JULY 25th to SEPT. 12th

PAGEANT OF TANNHÄUSER

Performances : Mondays & Thursdays.        Seating for 6,000 Spectators.

**Carrick's Popular Pierrots**

Carrick's Popular Pierrots in 1905. Tom Carrick was originally part of Sidney James's Strolling Players but left them to form his own troupe in the 1890s. He was a master at audience participation specialising in rhymes and verses which started slowly and accelerated mercilessly leaving the audience helplessly tongue-tied. An example is *He knew all about etymology, Hebrew, Shebrew and phrenology, Syntax, tin tax, hob-nailed boot jacks...*

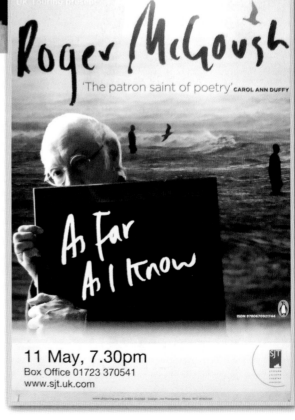

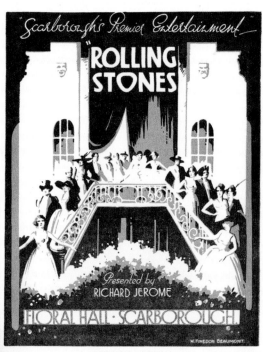

SEASON—1938

**The Rolling Stones 1938 and 1965**
The 1938 Season Floral Hall programme featuring Richard Jerome's *Rolling Stones*. The other Rolling Stones made it to Scarborough on the 8 March 1965 when they performed two sets: also appearing on the bill were *Dave Berry and The Cruisers, The Checkmates, The Konrads, Goldie and The Gingerbreads* and *The Hollies*.

*Fol-de-Rols*

One of the 1920s cast of the *Fol-de-Rols*, regulars at the Floral Hall. They started in 1911 when George Royle's pierrot show on beach was transferred to the newly built Floral Hall. Royle adapted the group so that ladies wore crinolines and bonnets and the gentlemen wore 'Johnny Walker' type velvet coats and trousers and beaver top hats. He changed the name from *The Imps* to the *The Fol-de-Rols*'. They continued to perform up and down the country until the 1970s.

# CHAPTER 8
# BACK TO
# THE FUTURE

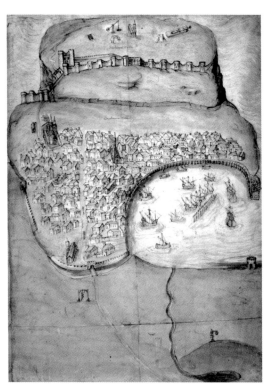

**Scarborough 1538**

In 1938 the Borough of Scarborough laid down some ambitious plans which would have involved considerable redevelopment of the town and its facilities. They were published in *The Borough of Scarborough: The Further Development of Scarborough* by S. D. Adshead and H. V. Overfield ; extracts from the book appear on the next pages. Unfortunately, the Second World War put paid to the plans. The map here is one of the town's earliest and was drawn for military use in 1538. It is now in the British Museum. The mural is in the Market Hall vaults. The proposed Peasholm Gap Bathing Pool on page 91 was one of two, the other being at Scalby Mills. Peasholm Gap would have been on the site of the children's boating pond and would accommodate 800 bathers with 106 cubicles; seating would accommodate 700 spectators.

The other photo shows the magnificent carvings on the facade of the houses opposite St Martin's on the Hill church.

*View from the Bridge*

*View from the Spa Bridge of the valley showing the roof of the Aquarium converted into gardens.* The Aquarium was opened in 1877 but a decline in popularity led to its conversion into Gala Land, an entertainment centre. The developers proposed demolishing it completely, replacing it with car parking, an ice rink and gardens.

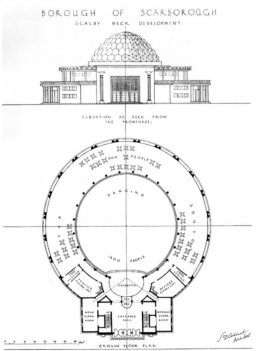

BOROUGH OF SCARBOROUGH
SCALBY BECK DEVELOPMENT.

ELEVATION AS SEEN FROM
THE PROMENADE.

GROUND FLOOR PLAN.

SCALBY BECK AMUSEMENT PARK, TEA LOUNGE
AND DANCE HALL.

**The 'Koh-i-noor' Hall**.

*Scalby Beck Amusement Park and Scalby Beck
Amusement Park, Tea Lounge and Dance
Hall.* The developers envisaged here '*an
illuminated pleasure park…swimming pool,
dance hall, children's boating lake, and the
present Scalby Mills Hotel developed into
an attractive open air cafe or beer garden in
continental lines*'. The domed terrace would
'*shine like an enormous jewel*' and '*might be
appropriately termed the 'Koh-i-noor' Hall*'.

94

**A New Olympia**
Here the idea was to demolish the current *'flimsy building'* and replace it with something neater and more commodious: indoor swimming pool, dance hall-cum-conference hall for 1,500 delegates, restaurant with roof garden.

Remembrance from Scarborough…
*White House covered swimming pool.* This low level sports and social centre below Crescent Gardens was intended to complement the adjacent Medicinal Baths which themselves were to be improved to include sea water slipper baths and sun rooms. White House would feature a sea-water swimming pool, gymnasium and squash and badminton courts. Much of the proposed redevelopment was based on the firm belief that the swimming pool was the thing of the future, due largely to the 'uncertain' and inconvenient nature of sea-bathing and because *'the days of the old bathing machine drawn by a horse to the edge of the sea is almost a thing of the past'.*